KU-440-598

Contents

Some words are printed in bold, **like this**. You can find out what they mean in the glossary.

What is Judaism?

Judaism is one of the oldest of the religions whose members believe in a single God. It was founded over 3,500 years ago in the **Middle East** when God made a **Covenant**, or promise, with Abraham. Abraham is considered to be the father of Judaism. For Jews, Israel is the land promised to them by God and today over 40 per cent of the world's Jewish population live there.

Beliefs and worship

Jews believe in a two-way relationship with God. While God promised to look after the Jewish people and give them the land of Israel, they promised to follow God's laws. This relationship is established in the Torah, the most important sacred text of Judaism. It is written in **Hebrew**. Jewish life centres on family and community.

Stories from Faiths

JUDAISM

Gina Nuttall

ALIS

www.heinemannlibrary.co.uk
Visit our website to find out more
information about Heinemann
Library books.

To order:

☎ Phone +44 (0) 1865 888066
📄 Fax +44 (0) 1865 314091
💻 Visit www.heinemannlibrary.co.uk

Heinemann Library is an imprint of Capstone Global Library Limited, a
company incorporated in England and Wales having its registered office
at 7 Pilgrim Street, London, EC4V 6LB – Registered company number:
6695582

"Heinemann" is a registered trademark of Pearson Education Limited,
under licence to Capstone Global Library Limited

Text © Capstone Global Library Limited 2008
First published in hardback in 2009
Paperback edition first published in 2010

The moral rights of the proprietor have been asserted.

All rights reserved. No part of this publication may be reproduced in any
form or by any means (including photocopying or storing it in any medium
by electronic means and whether or not transiently or incidentally to
some other use of this publication) without the written permission of the
copyright owner, except in accordance with the provisions of the Copyright,
Designs and Patents Act 1988 or under the terms of a licence issued by
the Copyright Licensing Agency, Saffron House, 6–10 Kirby Street, London
EC1N 8TS (www.cla.co.uk). Applications for the copyright owner's written
permission should be addressed to the publisher.

Designer: Harleen Mehta
Picture Researcher: S Kripa
Art Director: Rahul Dhiman
Client Service Manager: Aparna Malhotra
Project Manager: Smita Mehta
Lineart: Sibi N Devasia
Colouring Artists: Subhash Vohra, Danish Zaidi, Ashish Tanwar
Originated by Chroma Graphics (Overseas) Pte Ltd
Printed and bound in China by CTPS

ISBN 978-0-431-08224-0 (hardback)
13 12 11 10 09
10 9 8 7 6 5 4 3 2 1

ISBN 978-0-431-08231-8 (paperback)
14 13 12 11 10
10 9 8 7 6 5 4 3 2 1

British Library Cataloguing in Publication Data
Nuttall, Gina
    Judaism. – (Stories from faiths)
    296
A full catalogue record for this book is available from the British
Library.

Acknowledgements

We would like to thank the following for permission to reproduce
photographs (t = top, b = bottom, c = centre, l = left, r = right, m =
middle): Howard Sandler/ Shutterstock: 4t, Stavchansky Yakov/
Shutterstock: 5b, Photo Researcher/ Photolibrary: 7tr, Howard Sandler
Photography/ istockphoto: 8tl, Ted Spiegel/ Corbis: 11tr, Motimeiri/
istockphoto: 12tl, Denideni/ Dreamstime: 14tl, Ankevanwyk/
Dreamstime: 17tr, Pietro da Cortona/ The Bridgeman Art Library/ Getty
Images: 18tl, Nathan Benn/ Alamy: 21tr, ArkReligion.com/ Alamy: 22tl,
Jewish School/ The Bridgeman Art Library/ Getty Images: 25tr, Joe
Dalton/ Alamy: 26tl, Howard Sandler/ Shutterstock: 28tl.

Q2A Media Art Bank: 6–7, 8–9, 10–11, 12–13, 14–15, 16–17, 18–19,
20–21, 22–23, 24, 26–27, 29.

Cover photograph of a child reading the Torah reproduced with
permission of Bill Aron/ Photo Researchers/ Photolibrary.

We would like to thank Q2AMEDIA for invaluable help in the
preparation of this book.

Every effort has been made to contact copyright holders of material
reproduced in this book. Any omissions will be rectified in subsequent
printings if notice is given to the publishers.

Disclaimer

All the Internet addresses (URLs) given in this book were valid at
the time of going to press. However, due to the dynamic nature of
the Internet, some addresses may have changed, or sites may have
changed or ceased to exist since publication. While the author and
publishers regret any inconvenience this may cause readers, no
responsibility for any such changes can be accepted by either the
author or the publishers.

ABERDEENSHIRE LIBRARY & INFO SERV	
3004344	
Bertrams	23/02/2010
J296	£6.99

Every week Jewish families observe the Sabbath (the day of rest and worship) from sunset on Friday until it is dark on Saturday evening. They worship together in synagogues and their spiritual leaders are called **rabbis**.

Jewish stories

Judaism has a strong tradition of story-telling. It is through stories from the Hebrew Bible (the Old Testament, which contains Jewish laws and traditions) that Jewish ideas and beliefs are taught and passed down to new generations of Jewish children. The Hebrew Bible speaks of the "children of Israel" and, although Jewish people now live all over the world, they feel united in one big family. No matter where they are, the stories they tell and read celebrate their shared heroes and history. You can read some of these stories in this book.

The Western Wall, in Jerusalem, is a holy place where Jews come to pray.

Abraham's Test

Long ago, the people of Haran worshipped many gods. However, there was one man among them who was different. Abraham believed in only one God.

One day, Abraham heard God's voice commanding him: "Leave this place, Abraham! Go to a new land that I will show you. I promise that this new land will belong to you and your children."

Abraham left the land he knew to go to an unknown **Promised Land**. The journey was long and hard, but he trusted God and God looked after him well.

"Children? How is that possible?" laughed Abraham. "I am already an old man of seventy-five and I have no children."

"Look up at the night sky," God replied. "If you can, count all the stars. That's how many children and heirs you will have."

Abraham was puzzled, but his faith in God was so strong that he believed him. With his wife, Sarah, Abraham left Haran and journeyed to the Promised Land. However, many years passed and the couple were still childless. It seemed as if God had forgotten his promise.

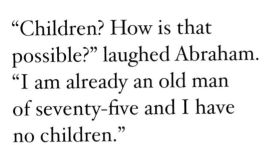

▲ Torah scrolls are handwritten on parchment, a stiff material made from goat or sheep skin. The Hebrew text is read from right to left.

The Torah

The most holy books of the Jewish people are the first five books of the **Hebrew** Bible, which are referred to as the Torah. The story of Abraham comes from Genesis, the first of the five books. Torah scrolls are kept in highly decorated covers. A pointer called a yad is used to follow the text, because the writing in the Torah scrolls cannot be touched directly with the hands or fingers.

▲ The shofar is one of the earliest instruments used in Jewish music.

Rosh Hashanah

The story of Abraham is read on Rosh Hashanah, the Jewish New Year. It reminds Jews of Abraham's willingness to **sacrifice** his son, proving his faith in God. On the Jewish New Year a ram's horn, called a shofar, is blown. The horn itself is a symbol of the ram that was sacrificed instead of Isaac, and the horn's trumpeting sound reminds Jews to start **repenting** before Yom Kippur, ten days later.

Then, one day, three strangers arrived at Abraham's home. They ate and drank with Abraham and Sarah and, before they left, one of them said, "Next year Sarah will have a son." Sarah laughed in disbelief.

The next year Sarah and Abraham did have a son! And Sarah laughed again – this time because she was so happy. Abraham and Sarah called their son Isaac, which means "laughter".

God watched Isaac grow up and saw how dearly Abraham loved him. "It is time now," thought God, "to test Abraham's obedience."

"Abraham," God commanded, "go up the mountain and offer Isaac to me as a sacrifice."

Abraham's heart nearly broke. The thought of losing Isaac filled him with deep sadness. But Abraham trusted God and did as God commanded. He took Isaac up the mountain and prepared a fire.

Just as he was about to place Isaac on the fire, he heard the voice of God's angel. "Stop, Abraham! God does not want Isaac to die. He was testing you."

Abraham wept with relief and hugged his beloved son. God had tested the strength of Abraham's faith and Abraham had passed the test.

The angel of God appeared before Abraham and Isaac and revealed God's plan.

Freedom at Last!

There was once an evil Egyptian **pharaoh** who feared the people of Israel. Since the time of Abraham, the **Israelites** (or **Hebrews**, as they are also known) had grown in number and many of them lived in Egypt.

"If they continue to grow, they may rise against us and take over the land," the pharaoh said. So he made them into slaves and ordered that all their boy babies be killed.

But one determined Israelite mother was not going to let that happen to her baby. She wrapped him warmly in blankets and hid him in a basket by the River Nile.

What luck! That morning when the pharaoh's daughter came down to the river to bathe, she noticed the basket floating in the reeds. "How strange! Go and see what it is," she asked one of her servants.

Moses' mother watched from a hiding place to see that he was safe.

Imagine their surprise to see a tiny baby inside! The pharaoh's daughter knew instantly that this beautiful little boy was a Hebrew baby, but she took pity on him. "This child will become my own and I will call him Moses," she said. So Moses was brought up as the son of the pharaoh's daughter – but he always knew in his heart and mind that he was Hebrew by birth.

▲ A family celebrates Pesach together. They read the Haggaddah, the story of the Passover, before they begin their meal.

Celebrating Pesach

The story of Moses, and how he became the great leader who led the Jewish people from slavery to freedom, is celebrated during an eight-day festival called Pesach (or Passover, in English). At the beginning of Pesach, many Jews enjoy a special family service and meal called a seder in their homes. On the table is a plate with items of food that symbolise the Passover story.

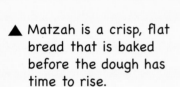

▲ Matzah is a crisp, flat bread that is baked before the dough has time to rise.

Festival food

During Pesach, Jewish people eat **unleavened** bread called matzah to remind them of when the Israelites left Egypt for freedom in such a hurry that their bread did not have time to rise. For the seder, three matzot (plural of matzah) are put on a plate. The middle matzah is broken and part of it is hidden. During the seder, children hunt for it. The winner receives a small prize.

It made Moses sad to see that his people were so badly treated. One day, he saw an Egyptian beating a Hebrew slave. Moses' anger got the better of him and he killed the bully. News of the slaying reached the pharaoh, who was enraged. "Find Moses and kill him!" he shouted. Fearing for his life, Moses fled from Egypt.

As time went on, Moses became a shepherd. One day, he was tending his flock when he saw a bush on fire. "How very strange!" he thought. Although the bush was in flames, it did not burn.

As Moses moved closer for a better look, he got the fright of his life. "Moses!" boomed God's voice from the middle of the bush.

"I have seen the pain of my people in Egypt. I want you to go back and ask the pharaoh to let my people go. I want you to lead them out of Egypt to the **Promised Land**."

Moses was nervous about facing the pharaoh. "I am just an ordinary man," Moses said to God. "Why would the pharaoh listen to me?"

"Do not be afraid," said God. "I will be with you."

God chose Moses to lead the children of Israel out of Egypt.

The Ten Commandments

I
Thou shalt have no other gods before me

II
Thou shalt not make unto thee any graven image

III
Thou shalt not take the name of the LORD thy God in vain

IV
Remember the sabbath day to keep it holy

V
Honour thy father and thy mother

VI
Thou shalt not kill

VII
Thou shalt not commit adultery

VIII
Thou shalt not steal

IX
Thou shalt not bear false witness against thy neighbour

X
Thou shalt not covet

▲ This is how an artist has imagined the Ten Commandments may have looked carved in stone.

The Ten Commandments

While the Israelites were camped near Mount Sinai, God called Moses to the top of the mountain. There He gave Moses two tablets, or blocks, of stone. On these were written a set of ten basic rules or commandments for people to live by. These rules explain what Jews' duties are to God and to other people.

So Moses and his brother, Aaron, stood before the pharaoh. "Let God's people go," they said.

The pharaoh scoffed, "They are my slaves. They are going nowhere!"

God decided to teach the pharaoh a lesson by giving Moses special powers to turn the pharaoh's river into blood. All the fish died and, oh, how the river stank! Still the pharaoh refused to let the Israelites go. So, God sent more **plagues**, but the pharaoh would not budge.

Finally, God sent a tenth plague – every first-born son in Egypt would die. Moses told the Israelites to mark their houses with blood so God would know to pass over those homes, keeping their children safe.

When the pharaoh realised what had happened, he shouted to Moses and his people, "Go! Leave Egypt now!" But as they reached the sea, they saw the Egyptian soldiers coming after them. The Israelites were trapped between the sea and the army!

"Stretch out your staff!" God told Moses, and when he did, something am____g happened. The sea parted, and the Israelit__ ____ to walk to the other side. Just as they _____ ___d and saw the sea close up again, drow__ ___ ____ ny.

At last, _____ ____ __ were free to go to the Promise__ ____.

___en the Israelites ___ched dry land, they ___ thanks to God and ___ses, God's servant.

ower Name:
__uch, __ anda

__wer Number: 63097

Barcode: 3004344

Inverbervie Library

David and Goliath

"Come on, I dare you!" roared the giant Philistine, Goliath, from the top of a hill. "I will beat any Israelite soldier in a fight!"

It was a time of battle between the **Israelites** and the **Philistines,** and every day Goliath shouted out his challenge. But not one of the Israelite soldiers would fight him. They were too afraid. Goliath was a huge and fearsome warrior.

Now it just so happened that on this day David, a shepherd boy, was bringing food to his brothers in the Israelite army. He heard Goliath bragging, yet he was not afraid. David was young, but he was strong and brave, and he believed in God. "I will fight that giant who challenges God's army," said David to Saul, the king of the Israelites. Everyone was stunned.

David defended himself, saying, "I may be just a boy, but I have killed both a lion and a bear that threatened my father's flock. Now I will kill this Philistine show-off who threatens our people."

Goliath was a giant and a fierce warrior, but David put his trust in God.

▲ This became the national flag of Israel when Israel was recognised as a country in 1948.

The Star of David

The symbol or emblem of the Jewish people is the Magen David (or Shield of David), also known as the Star of David. Although the origin of the symbol is linked to King David, there is no historical evidence for this. Today, the star with six points appears on the state flag of Israel.

▲ The original of this painting can be seen in the Vatican Museum, Rome.

David and Goliath in art

The battle between David and Goliath has inspired many artists throughout history. Pietro da Cortona, an Italian painter, painted his version in the 17th century. He chose to show the moment after David had knocked out Goliath with a stone from his sling. In this very dramatic picture, David is just about to kill Goliath with the giant's own sword.

"Go then," said Saul. "May the Lord be with you." He offered David his armour and sword, but David found them too heavy and uncomfortable.

"I cannot wear these," he said, stumbling. So he took them off and went to a small stream. There he chose five small, smooth stones. Armed with these, his sling and his staff, David went off to face Goliath.

The giant could not believe his eyes when he saw this boy in front of him. Was it a joke? "Do you think you have come to fight a dog with your pebbles?" raged Goliath.

But David was calm as he said to Goliath, "You are armed with a sword, spear and shield, but I do not need those things. I am armed with God's protection."

As Goliath lunged at him, David quickly took a stone from his bag and put it in the sling.

Round and round he swung the sling, sending the stone flying straight for its mark. It hit Goliath – THWACK – right in the middle of his forehead, and the giant fell down. With just a sling and a stone – and, of course, God on his side – David defeated the giant.

David killed Goliath and the army of the Israelites won a great victory over the Philistines.

Jonah Learns a Lesson

Long ago, in the land of Israel, lived a man named Jonah. One day, much to his surprise, Jonah heard God's voice. "Go to the city of **Nineveh**, Jonah. Tell the people there to stop being wicked. If they do not change their evil ways, I will destroy them."

The sailors did not want to throw Jonah overboard, but they had to save their own lives.

Now, the people of Nineveh were the dreaded enemies of the **Israelites**, and Jonah did not want to go there. "Why should I put myself in danger to warn my enemies?" he thought. So he ran away. He boarded a ship, hoping to hide from God.

That night, there was a terrible storm at sea. The ship rocked violently in the wild water. The sailors were afraid that it would sink and they would die. What could they possibly do to save themselves?

Jonah knew. He knew that the storm was his fault. He knew that God was punishing him for his disobedience. "Throw me overboard," Jonah told the sailors. "I am the one to blame."

So, reluctantly, they picked him up and tossed him over the side. Instantly the sea became calm.

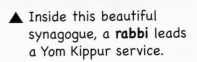

▲ Inside this beautiful synagogue, a **rabbi** leads a Yom Kippur service.

Yom Kippur

The story of Jonah is about obedience and forgiveness, and is read in synagogues on Yom Kippur. Known as the Day of Atonement, Yom Kippur is the holiest day of the Jewish year. Jews **fast** from sunset the day before, until darkness on the evening of Yom Kippur. This is to focus their attention on praying, and on remembering and feeling sorry for bad things they have done during the past year.

Down, down, down went Jonah into the deep sea. Surely he was drowning – but, no! Gulp! Jonah was swallowed whole by a big fish.

Jonah was inside that fish for three long days and nights. Then he prayed to God – and God heard him. At last, God spoke to the fish and it spat Jonah out onto dry land.

Jonah went straight to Nineveh and gave the people God's message. They listened, believed and **repented**. So God forgave them.

▲ A special prayer is said while lighting the yahrzeit candle. This prayer expresses a love for God and for those who have died.

Lighting candles

Just before Yom Kippur begins, Jews light candles to remember loved ones who have died. These special candles are called yahrzeit candles and burn for 24 hours. The flame of the candle symbolises the idea that the soul of the dead person still burns brightly in the life of the living person who is remembering him or her.

This made Jonah angry. He did not want God to forgive his enemies. He was afraid that if God did not destroy them, they would destroy the Israelites. He shouted at God and sat down outside the city to sulk. It was a hot day, so God took pity on Jonah. He made a bush to give Jonah some shade, and Jonah was thankful.

But the next morning, God sent a worm to eat the bush. Jonah became angry and felt pity for the withered bush. So God said to him, "Why are you angry? You show pity for a bush that grew one day and withered the next, a bush that you did not even plant. So, why can I not show pity for the many people of Nineveh?" Jonah then understood God's lesson: God's mercy and forgiveness are for everyone.

Although Jonah tried to hide from God, he eventually accepted God's will. So God gave him a second chance.

23

Esther, the Brave Queen

Long ago in Persia, King Ahasuerus held a contest to find a new queen. Young women from all over the kingdom were commanded to go to the palace to be presented to the king. However, when Esther walked in, that was it. The king was dazzled by her beauty and fell in love with her instantly.

King Ahasuerus beckoned Esther forward so that he could put the glittering crown on her head.

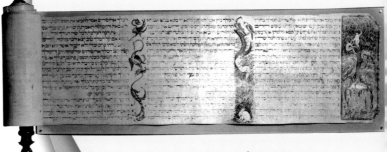

"She shall be my bride," the king announced – but he did not know that Esther had a secret.

Esther was an orphaned Jew, who had been raised by her cousin Mordecai. Because it was dangerous for Jews living in Persia at that time, Mordecai urged Esther not to reveal her Jewish identity. So she kept it to herself. Esther became queen and the king loved her very much.

One day, when Mordecai was outside the palace, he heard two men whispering. He thought, why would they be whispering if they weren't planning something bad? He hid and listened. They were plotting to kill the king!

"You must warn the king right away," Mordecai told Esther. So Esther did.

"Thank you for saving my life," the king said.

"It is not me you should thank," replied Esther, "but Mordecai."

▲ The story of Esther is written in **Hebrew** in this scroll, which is called a Megillah. It also contains some beautiful illustrations.

The Megillah

The story of Esther is told in ten chapters in the Megillah, the parchment scroll on which the biblical Book of Esther is written. It is read (usually twice) in synagogues during the festival of Purim. The Book of Esther is one of the books in the Hebrew Bible and the the Old Testament.

The king smiled and wrote Mordecai's good deed down in the record book.

Well, Mordecai might have pleased the king, but there was one man who hated him. That was evil Haman, the most powerful man in the kingdom besides the king. Haman was a man who thought he was better and more important than anyone else. When he walked down the street, he expected people to bow to him – but Mordecai would not. Mordecai would not bow down to anyone but God.

This made Haman absolutely furious. He wanted to get rid of Mordecai. Knowing that Mordecai was a Jew, Haman told the king that the Jews did not respect his laws and were plotting against him.

The king believed this lie and ordered that all the Jews be killed. (Remember, the king did not know that Esther was Jewish!)

▲ Children rattle graggers (noise makers) every time Haman's name is mentioned.

Purim festival

The festival of Purim is a reminder of how Esther saved the Jewish people in Persia long ago. *Purim* is Hebrew for "lots" as Haman **cast lots** to decide when to carry out his evil plan. Purim is usually celebrated in March and is one of the most fun of the Jewish holidays. Children dress up in costumes and read or act out the story of Esther.

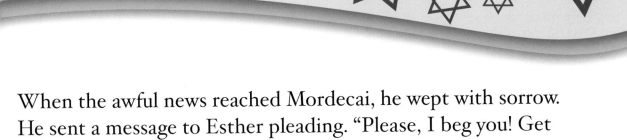

When the awful news reached Mordecai, he wept with sorrow. He sent a message to Esther pleading. "Please, I beg you! Get the king to change his mind."

Poor Esther did not know what to do. She wanted to save the lives of her people, but if she did, she would be risking her own life. In those days, even the queen could be put to death for going to the king without being summoned.

And even if she dared do it, how would the king react if she told him that Haman was an evil liar? And what would the king do when he found out her secret, that she was really Jewish? Esther spent a sleepless night seeking answers to these questions.

Esther was faced with a very difficult choice: reveal her secret or betray her people.

▲ The traditional filling for hamantashen is made with poppy seeds, but the recipe can be varied according to taste!

Hamantashen

A delicious Purim treat is triangular, filled pastries called hamantashen, which literally means "Haman's pockets". However, they are also called "Haman's hats" for Haman's three-cornered hat, or "Haman's ears" because his ears were his downfall when he listened to people who suggested he use his power to bring about the destruction of the Jews.

By morning, Esther had made her decision. "I will **fast** for three days," she told Mordecai. "Then I will go to the king."

Three days later, Esther stood trembling before the king. "What can I do for you, my dear?" asked the king lovingly. Esther breathed a small sigh of relief. She could have told the king everything there and then, but she wanted to choose just the right moment.

"I would like to invite you and Haman to a banquet I have prepared," Esther said.

The king and Haman enjoyed the delicious meal, unaware of what was to follow. When they had finished, Esther stood up and faced the king. "What is it, my dear?" said the king. "You look troubled."

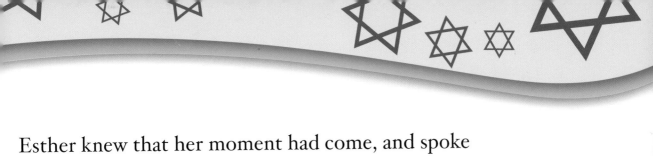

Esther knew that her moment had come, and spoke up bravely. "Please spare my life and those of my people who face death."

King Ahasuerus was shocked. "Death? What are you talking about? Who dares to do this thing?" he demanded angrily.

So Esther told him of Haman's evil plot. The king was furious and ordered that Haman be hanged that very day. Brave Queen Esther had saved the Jews and justice had been done.

The King ordered that Haman be hanged on the very gallows that Haman had built for Mordecai's death.

Glossary

cast lots – when a dice or other object is used to answer a question or to decide what to do next – for example, by picking a piece of paper out of a container with many pieces of paper

Covenant – the agreement made between God and Abraham about the future of the people of Israel

fast – go without food or drink for religious reasons

Hebrew – a Jewish person; the language in which the Torah and Jewish prayer books are written

Israelites – the people of Israel, descended from Abraham, with whom God made His Covenant

Middle East – a geographical region that includes Israel, Egypt, Syria, Jordan, Saudi Arabia, Iran, Iraq and other countries in southwest Asia

Nineveh – the capital city of the Biblical land of Assyria

pharaoh – an ancient Egyptian king or ruler

Philistines – group of people who were enemies of the Israelites

plague – disaster or serious misfortune

Promised Land – the land promised by God to the people of Israel as part of the Covenant

rabbi – person who leads Jewish people in worship. The word *rabbi* means "teacher".

repent – be sorry for and turn away from doing wrong things

sacrifice – give something up as proof of trust or faith

unleavened – made without yeast or other raising ingredient

Find out more

Websites

www.bbc.co.uk/religion/religions/judaism
Information about Judaism: beliefs, customs, history, holy days and people.

re-xs.ucsm.ac.uk/re/religion/judaism/intro.html
Links to introductory sites about Judasim.

www.torahschool.co.uk/links.htm
Introduction to Judaism – different articles and sites to explore.

www.virtualjerusalem.com/jewish_holidays/vjholidays.html
Information about the different Jewish festivals throughout the year.

Books

The Children's Illustrated Jewish Bible by Joseph Potasnik
Publisher: DK Publishing, 2007

Talking About My Faith: I Am Jewish by Cath Senker
Publisher: Franklin Watts, 2005

This is My Faith: Judaism by Holly Wallace
Publisher: Ticktock, 2006

Where We Worship: Jewish Synagogue by Angela Wood
Publisher: Franklin Watts, 2005

Index